STAINED GLASS ART

Religious & Abstract Coloring Book

Angelic Christian Designs, Mosaic Cross Patterns, Jewish, Decorated Abstract Windows- For Teenagers & Adults

Rachel Mintz

Images used under license from Shutterstock.com

Copyright © 2018 Palm Tree Publishing - All rights reserved.
No part of this publication may be reproduced, distributed, or transmitted in any form or by any means, including photocopying, recording, or other electronic or mechanical methods, without the prior written permission of the publisher, except in the case of brief quotations embodied in critical reviews and certain other noncommercial uses permitted by copyright law.

Join Our Coloring Books VIP Group
Members Get Giveaways, Deep Discount Offers,
Win Prizes – Visit Site To Join (It's Free)

www.ColoringBookHome.com

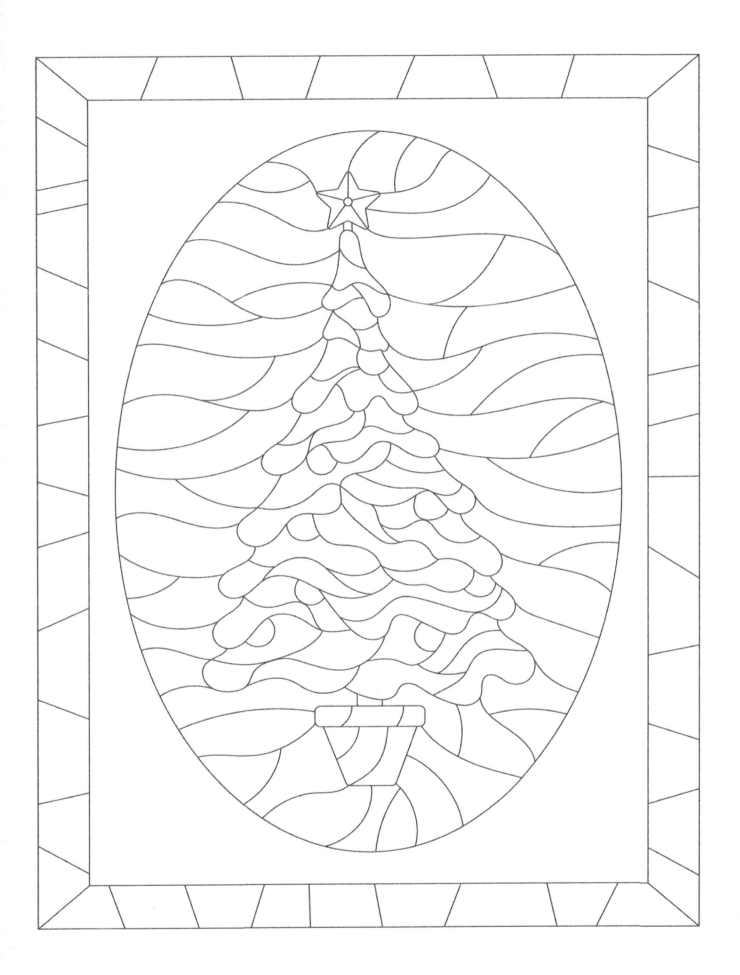

Thank you for coloring with us

Please consider to rate & review

More Coloring Books For You at Amazon:

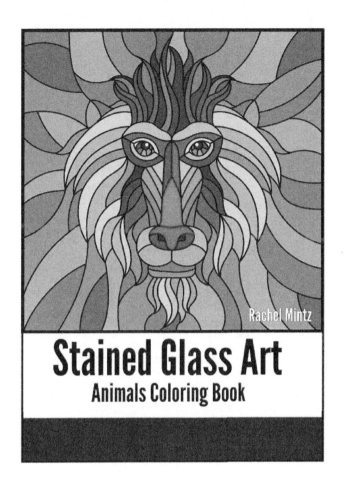
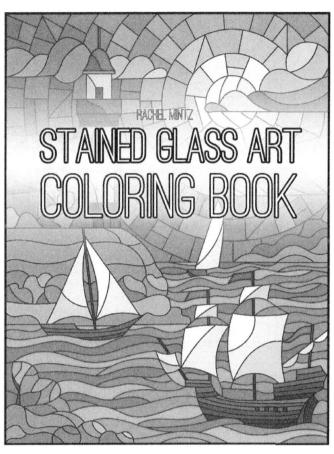

Join Our Coloring Books VIP Group
Members Get Giveaways, Deep Discount Offers,
Win Prizes – Visit Site To Join (It's Free)

www.ColoringBookHome.com

Thank you for coloring with us

Please take a moment to add a review at Amazon

Printed in Great Britain
by Amazon